# Advance Praise

"WOW!!! I could have not said it better myself. To read this, see you the other week, listen to you talk about the people aspect of business... You've grown so much and what a role model for others and your book. This is really a story of your career written in a way to help others along their journey. Bravo!"

BILL PALLETT, WJ PALLETT AND ASSOCIATES

"Serious congratulations - it is a good read, contains lots of advice and tips, and is not an academic or research piece (that is meant as a compliment). I mean it when I say that I enjoyed it."

MARTIN TIPLADY, PREVIOUSLY HR DIRECTOR FOR THE METROPOLITAN POLICE SERVICE

"Eugenio Pirri takes you on a wonderfully personal journey as a new breed of people-centric leaders. It's a pragmatic page-turner with values, purpose and legacy at the core. I highly recommend it. You will be a better people leader for it."

MARTYN DICKER, DIRECTOR OF PEOPLE & LEARNING, THE PRINCE'S TRUST

"Drawing on lessons learned throughout a highly successful career, Eugenio Pirri has produced an invaluable guide for those who aspire to be effective 'people leaders'. His approach is truly refreshing. Rather than mimicking others or adhering to prescribed leadership models, Pirri urges us to live by our values, express our authentic selves and to seek out organisational cultures within which we can flourish. In addition, he provides a step-by-step formula for attracting high calibre people, developing their talents and, ultimately, delivering business success."

DONALD SLOAN, HEAD OF SCHOOL –
OXFORD SCHOOL OF HOSPITALITY MANAGEMENT
AT OXFORD BROOKES UNIVERSITY

"This is a well written and thoughtfully structured book that takes the reader on a journey through which key information is imparted to them. Great for aspiring or existing 'People Leaders.' I love the way the chapters build in natural progression, this enables the reader to grasp a concept and then build on it logically with the next. The book is brought to life by Pirri's personal experiences and stories and help the reader connect with the content."

KAREN BEVAN, HR DIRECTOR RIVER ISLAND
(HR DIRECTOR OF THE YEAR 2015, HR EXCELLENCE AWARDS)

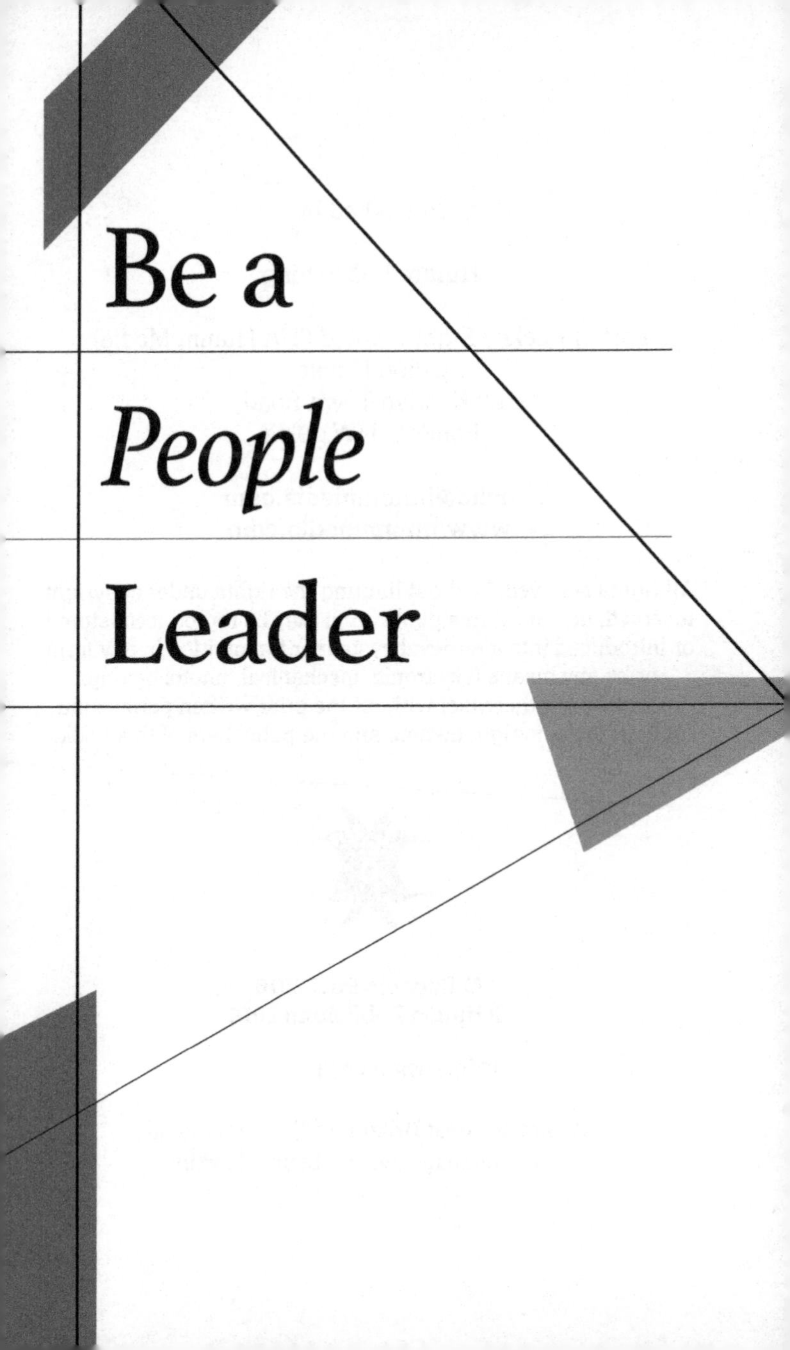
Be a
People
Leader

Published by

**Humm Publishing**

Part of Rockey Eight Limited (T/A Humm Media)
Union House,
20 Kentish Town Road,
London, NW1 9NX

**hello@hummmedia.com**
**www.hummmedia.com**

ISBN: 978-0-9934271-2-1

Printed in Great Britain by TJ International
Cover and page design: Laura Hawkins

# Be a *People* Leader

*A sustainable framework for achieving your full leadership potential*

Eugenio Pirri

*This book is for everyone I have had the pleasure to work and interact with throughout my career. Each of our interactions has helped me become who I am today and without that I could not have written this book.*

*I would like to thank my many mentors, both known and unknown, for their guidance, wisdom and setting the right examples.*

*And to my parents, who have since departed, for their support and teaching me the importance of being kind and treating people with respect, always.*

# A quick word before we begin...

I consider myself to be rather lucky.

Early in my life, I worked out the type of career I wanted, which, for many people, never happens. I knew I wanted to do something that involved people. People fascinate me; finding out about them is my hobby, you could say. I'm curious by nature, so I used to – and still do – watch people and learn about them, to ascertain what makes them tick, what enables them to grow, how they develop themselves. I have always asked people questions, intrigued to know more and to understand the human species better.

I was also fortunate to be allocated a mentor at work when I was quite young. My first was assigned to me when I was just 18 years old, another when I was 20 and a third when I was 23. I also had an array of unofficial mentors who didn't even realise I saw them as such. These were people whom I would watch and evaluate to try to understand what got them going in the morning; how they worked with their teams; what they did to move forward; how and why they made decisions. Not every mentor needs to be informed they are a 'mentor'.

Combine these early mentors with the range of training programmes I've been through – locally and internationally (from world-renowned organisations to the inspirational one-man-band down the street) and you'll see that I have been blessed with access to an array of different perspectives, thoughts, opinions and ideas around what it takes to lead people, enable people and empower people.

I have also experienced unlucky times, times when I've made mistakes – big ones and really useful ones. I've learned from each and every mistake; they've allowed me to change direction at certain points, or stay true to the course at others.

This shaping and exposure to the realities of business throughout my career, with positions ranging from a manager at McDonalds to a vice president of people and organisational development, has helped me become the people leader I am today. It has helped me gain a clear picture of who I am, what my path is and how I can continue to grow.

Because being a great people leader starts with you. I've always believed that you cannot grow as a person, grow your career, or grow your life to the point that it is almost limitless, until you truly understand who you are. It's not always about breaking down walls and going through them. Sometimes you need to go around the wall. You may just need to turn around and look at a different one.

You only realise this when you know yourself. It's about knowing where you can and cannot grow; knowing what it will take for you to change; knowing your limitations. Only then can you arm yourself with the right support, resources, tools and information to achieve your leadership potential.

And that's why I'm writing this book: in the hope that a reader, like yourself, will gain greater insight into who they are, enabling them to move forward. Because anyone can become a great people leader – whatever their style or their way – if they develop the right framework to begin with.

So read this book as if you're building something. I like to think of it as each reader working towards their masterpiece: each chapter should build on the previous one, adding a new layer or facet to their leadership framework.

The early chapters will help you focus on yourself – who you are, what you want to achieve and your purpose in life. Your own values will be crucial in planning your career and in understanding which would make the best employer for you. It will underpin your leadership style, your framework and the strategies you develop and implement throughout your career.

Strategies ensure the long-term success of the organisations in which we work, so the second part of this book is dedicated to helping you develop, enhance – and most importantly execute – strategies. All strategies grow from formulae or frameworks and we will look at how you, as an individual, can design your own frameworks and make sure they are supported by a robust people strategy, to ensure buy-in from colleagues and to make them sustainable.

Finally, we will explore how leadership improves with time, like a fine wine, and look at ways to progress your people leadership aspirations, take the next step in your career and leave a lasting leadership legacy.

Please read this book with an open mind. Dip in and out of it. It's not a 'how to' book, I'm not preaching about what you must and must not do to be a leader.

No, it's a practical resource to help you build your personal leadership style. Use the spaces provided to jot down notes. Really consider the questions posed and write down your thoughts. Carry the book with you, refer to it if in doubt, and witness yourself make the transition from reader… to people leader.

# Contents

# Introduction

People are the lynchpin of any business, and success or failure hinges upon them.

'People' are our staff; our customers; our suppliers; our introducers; the individuals who recommend us through word of mouth; our communities; our critics and defenders; our lifeblood.

Yet, in business, the idea of a company having a 'people strategy' is a relatively new concept. It evolved out of cold employee welfare and industrial relations, through the 'tissues and issues' phase of inward-looking personnel departments, and through the pseudo-strategic business-focused phase of human resources in the 1990s and early 2000s.

World-class 'people strategy' is being spearheaded by a new breed of leader. Their strategy is creative, disruptive, forward thinking, fiercely competitive – but equally collaborative.

And it's not necessarily coming from those with a life-long career in HR.

The leader of the future brings innovation, empathy, assertiveness, astuteness and, perhaps most importantly, a sense of humour. People leadership – if you can get it right – is a transferable skill. Those who master the art can go on to great things, taking their careers in directions, and achieving things, they might never have thought possible.

But people leaders need to prove their worth by stretching and provoking the business, as well as raising the game considerably in terms of demonstrating the return on investment of HR interventions.

The good news is that as the 'new breed' of HR leadership has begun to prove its worth to the board, customers and employees. The perception of HR has evolved dramatically, especially over the past five years, and we, as people professionals, should be proud of this. It feels as if there has been a seismic shift in the way in which business views people-centric leadership, and a growing realisation that it can truly add value to the bottom line. In the right environment, the new breed of leaders can be empowered to take risks to transform themselves and their businesses. They can lift their heads above the proverbial parapet to innovate, disrupt, think outside the box and to collaborate with other departments.

Surely this is a risk worth taking?

What is the core quality of the new breed of leader: strategic business expertise or operational people excellence? Most people would say the latter – you cannot furnish your house until you've plastered the walls, after all. On the other hand, one could argue that an excellent operations system could not be devised by someone who has little understanding of the workings of their business and the wider economy.

There are a couple of things that make people strategy a bit of a business anomaly.

First, as I have already highlighted, 'human resources' departments are a relatively new concept in business. Marketing, finance and operations have had years to develop themselves, yet HR – at least in the guise it currently adopts – is the 'new kid on the block', having only really come into existence in the 1990s. 'People leadership' only entered the equation within the past 10-15 years.

Second, the HR department is like a microcosm of the entire company. Not everyone in an organisation of any size will be affected by its advertising campaign or know about its turnover. And every employee will care about their career trajectory, their rewards and benefits and their terms and conditions. They all ultimately want to like their jobs, to feel engaged and valued. People strategy touches every employee, whether they consciously realise it or not. It follows, then, that HR has to understand the workings of the entire business from finance to front line; from boardroom to back office.

In order to unveil a leadership masterpiece, an aspiring leader must first have perfected basic operations, and that means knowing the business inside out and being spot on when it comes to policy.

However, many directors to whom I speak have 'fallen' into HR after being identified as excellent managers. At the same time, the industry is bottom-heavy with highly qualified 'HR careerists' with little experience in commerce and entrepreneurship.

In order to develop the stars of tomorrow and future-proof business, a new conversation is required about nurturing people-centric leaders.

And that conversation starts here.

# *Chapter* ONE

# Chapter 1

## Laying the foundation of your leadership framework: what do you stand for?

I gained my first leadership role at the age of 15. It's true. I was a team leader – and later one of the managers – of a McDonald's restaurant in British Columbia, Canada, when I finished school, and I was awarded 'manager of the year' and other such accolades three times during my three years with the company. There I was, a teenager, managing people, some of whom I went to school with, others who were the same age as my parents and grandparents. But I was learning the whole time. Mind you, I didn't really know what sort of leader I wanted to be until at least ten years into my career.

I think it's important for everyone to start considering the type of leader they want to be, and the framework they will use – both to develop themselves and their businesses – from the outset of their career, regardless of whether leadership is a personal aspiration or not. I say 'consider' not 'decide' because asking the big questions too early in your working life might not throw up the right answers. You'll need a bit of experience to be able to put your leadership style into context.

Asking yourself what type of leader you would like to be sounds like a really easy question: "I want to be a great leader" or "I want to make a difference", might be the first answers that come to mind. But to answer it intelligently, you need to know yourself – and this is a lesson I learned the hard way, relatively late on in my career.

In fact, if you were to ask you *now* what a good leader look likes, the sort of leader you would like to be and where you would like to end up, your answers might be different a year on, or even by the time you've finished reading this book.

Leadership can be defined in a lot of ways however the easiest is to define it emotionally. The best leaders don't have just one 'style' of leading. They have a few approaches up their sleeves. How they lead in success will be different to how they lead in change and conflict. And a quick note on this. Change and leadership go hand in hand, so being able to lead within it is something which must be mastered. It's no longer a choice given the world we now live in and people's expectations.

Empathy is an important quality – though so is the ability to make quick and difficult decisions, when too much empathy could cloud your judgement.

Having said that, people can only be one thing at a time and it's not always possible to make a tough decision while being empathetic. A leader may be described as "a tough person", "too friendly" "cold" or "too soft". However, great leaders are able to 'take the temperature' of a particular situation and know how to behave. Great leadership is a balancing act that is honed and crafted throughout a career. I'll return to this in chapter three, but essentially it's about drawing upon different emotions at different times.

Understanding who you are is the key to achieving this balance. It helps you to piece together your leadership formula and to begin building a world-class people strategy.

## VALUES FIRST

Before you think about how you should lead, where you should lead or even whether you want to lead, you need to clarify your own values.

Your values will be the paints with which you colour your career.

Talking about values has become something of a cliché, in the business world at least, but this is so wrong. Values define each and every one of us, whether we realise it or not. It has always been important to me to understand my own values, in order to make sense of the opportunities and challenges I have faced during my career.

Here are my values (you will have a chance to list your own later):

- **Passion:** I am passionate about what I do and I want to work with passionate people. I believe it's absolutely fine to be emotional at work. It's natural to grow excited about a project you're working on or to feel upset if something goes wrong in the workplace. Passion doesn't have to be reserved. Passionate people really care about what they're doing – they allow people to see the real 'them' and this is effective for building trusted relationships. It can also be healthy to argue and disagree at work – it helps you learn.

- **Honesty:** Openness and transparency are vital. Each day involves making decisions. Sometimes those decisions have a significant impact on what we do and creates a legacy that we don't recognise until later. Therefore, it is vital to act with integrity when making decisions. Honesty may lead to uncomfortable conversations but you will feel a great sense of relief knowing that your words, feelings, emotions and actions are truthful. This also means being honest about your own mistakes and expecting to give, and receive, genuine feedback.

- **Adaptability:** I like working in evolving cultures. I thrive on change and trying new things, so I like organisations that are not resistant to this, not stuck in a rut. This also means acknowledging different personality traits and adapting to personalities and cultures. One of my pet peeves is putting people into 'boxes' based on personality type; for example, 'introvert' or 'extrovert'. Yes, knowing that somebody has introvert or extrovert characteristics has its benefits, but assuming that a person will not be able to reach a certain level, or fulfil a task, because of these traits is wrong. Everyone is adaptable and everyone can achieve great things – it's about what's important to them.

- **Loyalty:** I'm loyal; that's me in a nutshell. Nothing makes me happier then developing relationships with others. I have been told that I can be quite intense in this value, as I reach out to people, stay in contact with them and develop friendships and partnerships. I love in a way that works for some and not for others. For me, loyalty is both an emotion and a way of behaving. I feel strongly about wanting to be more than a 'connection' on social media and I believe that, in the people world, this is essential.

So you see, my values define not just me, but how I interact with my colleagues and my peers, as well as my approach to the working environment. If you fake or hide your values, they will still shine through, and this is why you will not be successful in an organisation that doesn't share or appreciate your values.

The British Army is a great example of values in action. The army has developed recruitment slogans, such as "be the best" and is very clear about how it wants the public, and potential recruits, to view it. But in spite of this, everybody has his or her own idea of the army and what it stands for, based on his or her own personal values around conflict, pacifism, patriotism and so on.

Another example is the supermarket brand, Sainsbury's, which has come up with five values that are inherently connected to its growth plan. I know this because I spotted a gigantic mural highlighting values when I last popped into Sainsbury's to grab a sandwich.

Sainsbury's values are: best for food and health; sourcing with integrity; respect for our environment; making a positive difference to our communities; and being a great place to work.

In a challenging market, such as the supermarket sector, values and people combined create a competitive advantage. So when I walked out of that store, I felt really good that their brand values were displayed for all to see and confident that I would shop there again.

## PUTTING YOUR VALUES INTO THE CONTEXT OF YOUR CAREER

Thinking about your values and putting them into context will help you decide where to shop or eat, who to get to know and where to work.

My advice is to know and understand your values, to live by them and share them with anyone who will listen. Whether you work in a small, medium or large company, your values are the key to your growth as a person and as a business. The values of a business define how each and every decision should be made and if you, as an individual, don't share these values, you won't be able to be impartial. This will render you unable to make the right decisions for that organisation.

Organisational values are the conscience of a business, so it doesn't fall to its leaders to make the decisions, it falls to the values. Values are as much about understanding how and why decisions are made, as they are tools for making decisions.

If you can get your values straight in your head and use them as your rudder – both within your current role and when planning your career trajectory – the rest should fall into place.

## YOUR VALUES

Take some time to reflect on your values and how they affect your life. Think of yourself as a brand…

establish your unique selling point (USP). Your brand encompasses your values, your ethos, your beliefs and the things that make you unique.

### LIVING YOUR VALUES AT EVERY LEVEL

*On numerous occasions I've visited high-end stores selling luxury goods and have been made to feel as if they were doing me a favour by allowing me through their doors, rather than grateful for my potential custom.*

*However, I would imagine that the core values of such businesses are all about embracing their customers, caring about their needs and offering a level of service that matches the quality of the products they sell.*

*The problem is not that they lack values, but that the values have not been cascaded through the organisation. As leaders, it's our responsibility to bring values to life at every level and to ensure our people are guided by them, regardless of the money being spent by any individual customer.*

*If the company isn't doing a good job of following through on its values, then that's the responsibility of its leader. It's down to you.*

Some years ago, the concept of the 'cult of the leader' dominated management thinking. An excess of corporate disasters had led academics to question whether these were the fault of poor leadership, and the response was a wave of leaders raising their profiles and showing the world they had the grit and charisma to be the next Steve Jobs, Mark Zuckerberg, Arianna Huffington or Sheryl Sandberg.

But, while these leaders are certainly role models to millions, they're not obsessed with self-promotion. In fact, Zuckerberg shies away from the limelight, as did the late Steve Jobs.

Instead, what these leaders have in common is authenticity. They're not afraid to be themselves. Think about this in terms of a defining factor – what's your USP going to be? What can you bring to the board table or to your business that makes you valuable or interesting? If you deny yourself your authenticity and model yourself on another person's brand, you run the risk of being a corporate clone. I wouldn't wish that on anyone – in fact, if that's what your employer expects of you, you're in the wrong job.

What do you stand for and what do you reject? What do you and your difference represent? How can you make your differentiating factors useful to yourself and the organisation?

If you think about your career in terms of a painting, your values are the colours in your palette.

The term 'soul searching', sounds a bit 'free thinking' to me, but sometimes, taking the opportunity to consider questions like this can pay dividends, helping you to define what you want to do with your life and the message you want to project to your colleagues and to the world.

## Over *to* YOU:

*Take 10 minutes to consider your USPs and your values? Use the space below to list them. Then consider how you will use them throughout your leadership journey. Jot down your thoughts and reflect on them often.*

# *Chapter* TWO

# Chapter 2

## What role will skills and talents play in your framework?

I love to sing and I love art. Sadly, I will never be as good a singer as my fellow Canadian Celine Dion, nor will I ever paint like Pablo Picasso, no matter how hard I try. There I've said it.

And believe me, I try...

The statement on page 37 summarises, for me, the difference between skills and talent. I can take singing lessons or improve my painting skills but I will never have the natural talent of the artists I have mentioned. Skills can be taught; talent is inherent.

I define talent as everyone in any organisation. Talent is not confined to 'pools' as some experts might tell you. And talent does not merely mean people identified as having high potential. Talent is abundant and can be found throughout the business. It can be recognised in the people who champion your culture and live your organisation's values, whether at entry level or in more senior roles, on the frontline or behind the scenes. It is in those who will be the leaders of the future.

But I recognise the impact that the nurturing of talent has on people, in terms of improving their prospects; the impact on our communities of encouraging social mobility; the impact on our customers of providing them with world-class service; the impact on our companies of positioning them to grow exponentially; and on our sector, when we raise the profile of exceptional people.

**TALENT**

Individuals have innate talents. Too many organisations still fail to understand that some people are born with natural talents and others are not – talent cannot be created or forced. But, if you understand your own talents you will recognise with whom, and where, you can work well.

Over the years, through various talent assessments, I've discovered that I'm naturally a very strategic person; once I figured this out, I wanted to become more strategic and to learn more about it. This enabled me to develop strategy that got results.

ACCORDING TO GALLUP'S STRENGTHFINDERS REPORT, I AM:

1. **STRATEGIC** – *a 'big picture thinker', able to 'see the roadmap' and how to get to a destination*
2. **AN ACTIVATOR** – *good at getting things done, taking action on decisions, saying "let's start now"*
3. **A MAXIMISER** – *great is not good enough, I only accept excellence*
4. **A RELATER** – *with an ability to empathise with others and see things from different perspectives*
5. **FUTURISTIC** – *able to imagine what's over the horizon and to think about where we are going*

I also found out that while I'm capable of achieving 'harmony', it is not a natural talent of mine. I thrive on a little conflict in relationships and I don't expect my team members to be best friends. I understand the obsession with achieving harmony, but I think disagreement helps you learn (it's also one of the first things you learn in life, so why not embrace it?).

So, for me, there are degrees of talent. As individuals, we each have a range of qualities and talents, some of which will be stronger than others. Everything is about degrees and scales, so when it comes to talent, nothing is black and white; it's as much about considering and developing the talents you have that are further down the scale as those at the forefront of your repertoire.

Think about your natural talents; if in doubt, there are various online tests available from reputable companies such as Gallup, Dale Carnegie, Talent Q and iWam which can help you identify them. A quick search will help you track down the right tool for your needs.

## SKILLS

Unlike talents, skills can be learned or developed. Talent can also be enhanced (though you start from a slightly different base) but it cannot be instilled in a person or taught from scratch.

For instance, a waiter might be a natural at greeting diners and making guests feel welcome (talent), but still require training in how to provide silver service (skill). All skills can be taught – but to varying degrees. If you're naturally talented at singing, I can give you some training and you'll be amazing. But if somebody is not a natural singer, even with the same training, they will only attain a limited level of success. Just like a degree of talent, there is a degree of skill.

Anyone can be taught to paint, but not everyone will have their work displayed in the Tate Britain. Anyone can follow a recipe, but not everyone can decorate a cake with creative flair.

That is the difference between talent and skill.

There are two types of skill: hard skills and soft skills. I believe we spend too much time contemplating physical (hard) skills (such as writing, cooking or public speaking) and not enough time thinking about the emotional (soft) skills.

Soft skills are around empathy, caring, listening – anyone can be taught to listen, but some people are naturally 'good listeners'. So even when it comes to emotional skills it's important to stress that people start from different bases. You can teach anyone to study for a test, but if someone has talent in a particular area, that will influence the level to which they excel. They might be particularly numerate, literate, enjoy puzzles and so on. In the hotel industry, we teach people up to six different techniques for learning guests' names because different members of staff will find it easier to learn guests' names in different ways. One way may be finding out a guest's name and repeating it several times to yourself; another might involve associating a feature with that person (though don't pick something that can be changed, such as glasses). They both achieve the same result – making it easier to recall names – but people are able to choose the approach most suited to their preferred learning technique.

There are many people out there who say you can master anything by putting in 10,000 hours of practice; however, to my mind, it involves more than that. It's about determination, dedication, desire, being a futurist. It's about using your strengths to boost your skills. So if you know that your strength lies in research, use that strength to master your skill by studying, exploring and asking questions. If your strength is in strategising, create a strategy and action plan to achieve your goal. Use the tools available to you – don't just rely on practice.

## IN THE WAR FOR TALENT, IS IT TIME FOR PEACE?

In survey after survey, year after year, it is revealed that CEOs plan to adapt their talent strategy drastically in an effort to retain future leaders. These surveys imply that the "war for talent", a phrase coined by McKinsey back in the pre-recession noughties, is raging on. Experts refer to the current climate as a "heated labour market" in which employers are competing for top talent.

Some commentators have gone as far as to suggest that this "war is over and talent has won". But what does that even mean?

I have to question why employers and recruits are allegedly battling with each other, when there is so much competition facing both in the global recruitment market. Surely there is a way for both employers and recruits/employees to win?

Rather than being frightened of talent, employers – and that means you, as leaders – need to clarify the definition of talent in their own heads, to understand what it means in terms of their leadership framework and people strategy.

You have to look at yourself first, acknowledge your own values, talents and skills, then work out how you will use these in reality. This could be within your department, your discipline, country, continent or the world...

If you, as a leader, have not clarified your own definition of talent, you are going to find yourself confused when it comes to any facet of people leadership.

Take some time to think about your own talents and the talent of your organisation in terms of inclusion, diversity, ethics, values and your economic environment.

In any war, strategy and tactics are key to success and, in most cases, the simpler the strategy the more effective it will be. I have a simple, yet tactical, approach to hiring, developing and retaining the best people that is not all about analysing 'talent pools' or 'talent pipelines'.

An approach to talent should have the simple-but-vital remit of putting the right people in the right roles. This is the secret to delivering the best customer experience and to growing your business.

If, when hiring, you combine values-based talent attributes with alignment to company culture, your recruits, given the right learning, development and coaching, will achieve personal growth and success and ensure the growth and success of the organisation.

Taking my thoughts on skills and talent a step further, I believe that each of your employees, current and future, has a natural ability to achieve near perfect performance. You simply need match their ability to the right role or department.

If everybody is put in a position in which they are able to use their natural talents, understand their company's culture and receive ongoing learning and development, their potential for performance is limitless.

I use this formula as part of my HR strategy and conduct online talent assessments or face-to-face interviews to help identify the top performers. I look at who has the potential to execute a specific role, whether they are the right fit for our culture and what specific investment is required to help them grow.

The same is absolutely true for you as an individual. Once you're sure of your talents and skills and recognise the areas in which you could undertake further training to maximise your performance, you can thrive in an organisation – provided its corporate culture is right for you. Remember, you cannot succeed in an organisation where you cannot buy into its culture or share its mission and values.

## Over *to* YOU:

*Think about the skills in which you have undertaken training, and your natural talents, and work out how these could be used to enhance your CV and shape your career path.*

# *Chapter* THREE

# Chapter 3

## How would you define your leadership style?

Once you've defined your personal values, your skills and your talents as part of your framework, you can start thinking about your leadership style and putting together the things you've learned about yourself, your experiences and your career history.

## BUT WHAT IS LEADERSHIP?

Earlier, I mentioned that I was a team leader at the age of 15, working at a branch of McDonalds. This flies in the face of the popular perception of what a leader looks like: the older middle-class white male in an ivory tower, disconnected from day-to-day business.

Youth, race, sexuality and gender are not barriers (and should not be) barriers to leadership. And regardless of whether you want to be a team manager or business leader you can, and should, adopt the personality of a leader.

## LEADERSHIP AND PURPOSE

The one overarching thing I would say about leadership is that it has to have purpose. Once you know your purpose as a leader, that's when you move from being an adequate leader to an inspirational leader.

Let me give you an example. I went into HR at the age of 23, and by the time I was 26, I was an HR director. I recall receiving a letter from a woman I'd hired as a room cleaner at the previous hotel where I'd worked. When I recruited her, she had just moved to Canada and her English was basic, but she was an excellent cleaner, so I offered her the job. I didn't know it at the time, but the fact I'd employed her allowed her to sponsor her husband and children to join her. I offered her husband a job as a cleaner as well and, over the years, he worked his way up and became night manager of the hotel. The letter was telling me she was now in a position to leave her job and care for her children full time, something that would never have been possible had I not taken a chance on her.

This resonated with me and made me realise that, until then, I'd been looking at my job from a very functional perspective; I'd assumed I was there to hire people. Instead, I realised I was giving people an opportunity to live: to raise children, buy homes, gain citizenship, receive opportunities. This was a defining moment in my career, because it completely changed the way I viewed HR and people leadership. I identified my true purpose. From this point on, I knew why I was there. I was not only there to fulfil a job and affect profit and loss, I had a bigger purpose. This is what drives me and this is what helps me inspire others. It's why I get up and go to work every day.

Purpose is becoming increasingly important to workers. Research, including the *Deloitte Millennial Study 2016*, has found that the leaders of tomorrow want to work somewhere that not only aligns with their own values, but helps them to achieve a greater sense of purpose. To thrive in an organisation, you need to take the values that you identified earlier in this book and use them to define your purpose. It may be a little hazy when you start your career; however, if you use these values as your guiding force, you can choose an organisation with the right values, performance, development methods and engagement for you. This will be an organisation that helps you change your perception of work from a 'job' to 'a place where you can achieve purpose'.

Leadership without purpose is nothing more than fulfilling a function. We are not here to fulfil functions – we're worth more than that. When your role is greater than a function, you can achieve so much more. Then, and only then, will you become an inspirational leader. Leadership is about 'the things people see you putting out there' rather than 'what you think you're putting out there'. I refer back to my example of the army. Everyone has an opinion of what it's like to be in the army, regardless of how it brands itself as an employer. Individuals may love it, hate it, feel proud of it, scared of it and so on. The same is true of leadership. Your style is how people perceive you, and for that reason, it's really important to reflect on leadership. Too few people scrutinise their own style of leadership. They believe that, because they've won awards, achieved good results or are told they're good leaders, they must be performing well. In reality, it is only the success of your team that marks you out as a good leader – how team members are growing and what they are achieving – and how this aligns with the organisation's values and goals.

Great leadership is a combination of the following (and more):

- **Commercial acumen** – understanding how business works and how the functions of the organisation operate and come together. This is also about going a step further and understanding how your strategy ties into the overall vision and how it will deliver sustainable returns to the company. To boost commercial acumen and ensure everyone is 'on the same page' you must focus on improving yourself and the people with whom you're working.

- **Diplomacy** - being able to deal with people and manage them sensibly, sensitively and tactfully. This doesn't mean being reserved, your voice has to be heard. I always say "do your job like you're not afraid to lose it". It's about having strength and the courage of your convictions so that you say when things are going well and also when things can be improved. It's also about speaking up when things are bad or unethical, in a respectful way.

- **Leadership knowledge** - understanding how to get the best out of people. There are two elements to this. There's the commercial acumen which we have already discussed, and then there's the ability to understand people on a more human level; becoming a coach who leads by listening; using your knowledge of their talents and their interests to take advantage of opportunities that have been presented.

- **Operational excellence** – making sure the basics are in place and laying the ground work before launching a complex initiative. This means knowing what the 'game board' looks like and how your scorecard is set up. You need to know where you stand, what's important for you and what are you playing towards. It involves using external benchmarking in the right way, not just because you have access to it.

- **Strategy** – being able to set clear plans that are straightforward to execute, rigorous and measurable. This is different to being futuristic and having foresight, although these skills are also important in leadership.

- **Impact** – being able to set manageable targets and smash them (both for the business but also for yourself). First, you need to define impact, because it's not always about the bottom line. It could be the number of customers through the door, the number of transactions carried out or the retention of your people. Understanding what you truly want to impact, and what you choose to measure, will show you how to achieve sustainable success.

  If you again liken your career to a painting, the qualities listed above make up the palette upon which the paints, your values, are mixed. But the purpose, inspiration and soft skills we discussed in chapter two are the difference between 'adequate' and 'awesome'; they are the colours. The leaders who are inspirational are those who inspire others to be great. Inspirational leaders need the following qualities as well:

- **Kindness** – taking other people's feelings, needs and personalities into consideration and making them feel included and engaged; being able to relate to people. Empathy is a concept I simultaneously love and hate because it's virtually impossible to put yourself in someone else's shoes.

- **Openness** – being honest and transparent, talking with colleagues, seeking opinions, and promoting inclusiveness. Openness is also about people *seeing* that you are open. Many businesses have an open-door policy, and the doors may be physically open, yet very few go in. That's because what is being said isn't translating into the culture of the organisation. So you need to determine what openness is to you and how you incorporate it into your organisation.

- **Determination** – being committed to the mission, culture and values of the organisation and believing in the strategy. Remember, though, that determination is personal to the individual. Therefore, you need to decide what determination means to you: how do you show determination and how do you make sure people know you're in the race?

- **Ability to make tough decisions** – being decisive, even when you know your plan of action may be unpopular; having the conviction to stick by your decision, but having the empathy and transparency to communicate your strategy clearly.

- **Integrity** – accepting nothing but the best. It's about being relentless in the pursuit of quality, always aiming to go one better, pushing forward and making decisions that will enable long-term sustainability.

- **Accountability** – being able to take ownership of both the good and bad. This involves taking calculated risks and responsibility for errors. This is really a question of ethics: are you accountable for the decisions you make? Are the people around you accountable? Do you and they follow the code of conduct – always? You wouldn't steal a stapler outside of work, so why would you take one from your employer? Make sure your internal and external ethics are aligned.

And one more thing: in order to be a successful people leader, you have to be more than a little bit 'crazy'.

The 'ivory-tower dwelling leaders' with a purely profit-driven mindset will view employees who bring their emotions into the workplace as 'unprofessional' or weak. But people are more than figures on a spreadsheet. They are complicated. The growing trend of work/life integration, wherein people invest a large percentage of their time, energy and thought into their work, means that emotions will occasionally spill out.

Returning to the soft skills we discussed in chapter two, it takes an empathetic and understanding people champion to gauge which issues lead to loss of productivity and rectify them. If an employee cries at his desk, that doesn't make him incapable. It exposes a problem that needs to be addressed with sensitivity.

An emotionally intelligent leader or director is more likely to be able to manage these challenges.

Emotional intelligence (EQ), equates to a soft skill missing from the job descriptions of many CEOs. This type of intelligence is a core strategic imperative in directing the intangible and unpredictable feelings of the workforce; it renders inspirational directors not over-emotional, but effective.

At the other end of the emotional spectrum, according to Forbes at least, some of the world's best leaders are psychopaths. Forbes explains that "psychopaths may be charismatic, charming and adept at manipulating one-on-one interactions. Unfortunately, certain of these psychopathic qualities – in particular charm, charisma, grandiosity (which can be mistaken for vision or confidence) – are also qualities that can help one get ahead in business."

These are not the people-centric CEOs for whom we aspire to work (or wish to become) but they do walk among us and we have to interact with, and influence, other business leaders on their level.

Disruptive, innovative leadership strategies that shake up businesses and position them in a sustainable growth trajectory come from a blend of common sense and (a dash of) 'uncommon' sense. Innovation, by its very definition, brings new ideas, so be prepared to come up with suggestions that will raise a few eyebrows in your business. Have the confidence in your plan (supported by background research) to drive forward with it. This creativity, married with a healthy dose of pragmatism, makes for truly innovative practices.

After all, history tells us that some of the world's greatest visionaries were perhaps not recognised in their own lifetime; for example, Gauguin, Monet and Kafka, to name a few from the worlds of art and literature.

Let's describe the 21st century leader: "emotional and soft, yet a strategic hardliner; creative yet pragmatic; managing the books and the board, yet raising the bar with surprising ideas."

One could argue that a modern leader has to have a dual personality, to be multi-faceted, able to switch mindsets at the drop of a hat, expected to empathise with, and influence, every element of the business. This combination of qualities and approaches could drive anyone to distraction – but will not defeat the seasoned people professional.

So by "crazy", I don't mean "you'd have to be insane to do this job". I mean crazy in the sense that the more 'mentally interesting' among us are the ones that will thrive in leadership positions.

My advice is to celebrate and embrace the things that make you and your role 'weird'. These authentic qualities are what will differentiate you from the crowd, when the time comes to prove your worth.

## PERCEPTIONS OF LEADERS

Lots of books about leadership encourage readers to follow leadership role models. I believe this has led people to spend too much time trying to mimic others. I find it disturbing. I go to schools and speak at events and audiences seem to look up to me – and that's lovely – but unless you've walked a day in someone else's shoes you're only seeing their style from one perspective.

Any leader can say great things but you only see one side to them. My team has seen me on really awesome days and 'not so awesome' days and therefore would probably paint a different picture of me to those who have seen me on a stage with my pre-prepared presentation.

If you want to follow a role model, take them off their leadership pedestal and look at the things that make them unique as an individual, rather than considering what you do not have. Don't think about a leader and decide "I want to be them". Be cautious about that. Don't try to emulate them – they might have talents and skills that you don't have. They might have values that conflict with yours. They might be great at coming up with ideas but hopeless at executing them.

# Over *to* YOU:

*Consider inspirational leaders you admire and focus on their USPs. Jot these down below. Next, take a look at yourself; flick back to chapter one and remind yourself of all the things that make you authentic. Note these down. Think about the elements – whether operational excellence or EQ – on which you could work in order to take your leadership style from adequate, to inspirational, to awesome.*

# *Chapter* FOUR

# Chapter 4

## In what type of organisation would you thrive?

This is a tough one!

You may believe, in your own mind, that you would like to work for a particular organisation, but if it doesn't share your values, you won't thrive there. That's a given.

So how do you begin to search for the right organisation for you?

The best way to do this is to think about it in terms of your own framework and then map out your strategy. By now, based on chapters one, two and three, you should have considered your values, given some thought to your skills and talents, and from these, decided on a purpose for your career.

Now it's time to do your homework. Think about the jobs you would like to do and where you could find these jobs.

# Over *to* YOU:

*Use this space to write down your thoughts...*

Next, identify companies that appeal to you and employ people in roles which you fancy. Take some time to research their mission statements. For example, sports giant Nike's mission statement is "Just Do It", whereas the Ritz Carlton hotel chain's is "We are Ladies and Gentlemen serving Ladies and Gentlemen", so the cultures of these two organisations will be completely different. Whether you're applying for a role in marketing, HR or finance, your job will feel different.

There can even be huge variation within the same sector. Let's consider airlines: British Airways' mission statement is "To Fly, To Serve" whereas Virgin Atlantic's is "Unleash Your Mojo". Which culture is the best fit for you? Do you identify with legacy or modern?

# Over *to* YOU:

*List the types of company that best suit you here:*

MISSION STATEMENTS VARY FROM COMPANY TO COMPANY.

HERE ARE A FEW OF MY FAVOURITES:

- **GOOGLE** – *"to organize the world's information and make it universally accessible and useful"*
- **FACEBOOK** – *"to give people the power to share and make the world more open and connected"*
- **INNOCENT** – *"to make natural, delicious food and drink that helps people live well and die old"*
- **ZAPPOS** – *"to provide the best customer service possible"*
- **PATAGONIA** – *"to build the best product, cause no unnecessary harm, use business to inspire and implement solutions to the environment crisis"*
- **AMERICAN EXPRESS** – *"to be the world's most respected service brand"*
- **IKEA** – *"to create a better everyday life for the many people"*

Then, consider each organisation's corporate structure, corporate governance, how it is built and run, how it is portrayed in the press, and how it is perceived by the public.

From here the question you need to ask yourself is "how could I make a difference in this company?" In other words, as a leader, how could *you* add value to that organisation? Think about the leaders who are already there – how are they perceived? How do their values affect and navigate the direction the organisation is taking?

## THE REALITY OF WORKING FOR AN ORGANISATION

Once you *believe* you could work for a particular company, the next step is to investigate the reality.

When I go for a new role, I expect to be interviewed by two or three people. I then go and interview eight or nine people myself – sometimes without them even knowing. Find out as much as you can about an organisation. You need to experience a company before you know whether you will succeed there. At a job interview, an employer can tell you whatever they like or whatever they think you want to hear. You need to find out as much of the inside track as you can.

In the US, there used to be a television show where people who were buying a property could take an option of staying in that house for up to a week, to find out whether they could actually live there. It's 'try before you buy'. I don't see why we can't look at our careers in the same way.

See what people are saying about the business on social media. Read the review on employer rating sites such as Glassdoor, and customer feedback platforms like Trustpilot. Experience the business as a customer - go and buy a sandwich at a retailer you're interested in working for, stay the night at the hotel group you admire or phone a potential employer's call centre for a quote. If you want to get a feel for the business performance of the organisation then seek out their company accounts online. Do what it takes to get under the skin of the business; only then can you truly decide whether it's the right place for you.

## NOT QUITE 'YOU'?

I think that, in the right circumstances, it's absolutely possible to thrive in an organisation that's not 100% the right fit for you. You might feel passionate about the role, but note things that unsettle you or that you want to change. Think hard about the values of the organisation before you begin because whereas policies can be changed – values will be harder to alter. If you are still interested in joining, make sure there is an openness to change and that you would have sufficient voice to be able to make that happen – or at least be heard. You should also feel confident that the organisation would empower you.

## HOW LONG SHOULD YOU STICK IT OUT?

If you make a decision to take a job, then give it your all. I don't believe you should leave a job in less than 12 to 18 months. If your first three to six months don't go well, you won't yet have had enough experience to make a considered decision about your future there.

I once had a job I hated because of a poor line manager. I worked there for a year because I had made an obligation in my contract to give it my all and I did.

I was able to increase engagement scores and achieved what I was hired to do. After a year, I was out of there. I think there's something to be said for learning from working for poor managers, as much as you learn from great people. I know I will never be like the leader I left.

The best part… I was invited back to join the company two years later, at a higher level and with greater ability to make positive change! The moral of this story: you never know how paths may cross again so don't burn any bridges.

## Over *to* YOU:

*Where are you currently working? Take some time to map out your framework and the leadership direction within your present organisation.*

# *Chapter* FIVE

# Chapter 5

## What type of business do you want to create and how will you build that foundation?

If you've read this far, you'll know I like art analogies when describing leadership.

I've also talked about putting together a framework for your leadership excellence. So, I'll make the comparison again: if your values are the paints, and your leadership skills and talents are the palette and colours with which you're working, then your framework is both the initial drawings you'll do to sketch out your masterpiece and the brushstrokes you'll take to complete it.

Building a foundation for yourself in a business is like sketching and experimenting for the masterpiece you'll create in the future. In real terms, this is where individual leadership framework meets business strategy.

Before we get into the detail of turning your framework into reality, I would like to highlight five points that I believe are the keys to success in business. I want to share them with you before I go any further.

## 1. DO WHAT MAKES YOU HAPPY

There are so many people trying to tell us to be something we're not. For that matter, there are all too many people trying to be something they're not!

You are presumably in a job and a role because you have chosen it. So, with that in mind, stay true to yourself and work for an organisation that fits who you are and shares your values. If these are aligned, you have a chance to succeed and make a positive difference. However, while respecting your individuality, respect that of others as well – this will lead them to appreciate you and your decisions. Leaders can offer inspiration. How we act, what we do, how we listen, and the legacies we create are all within our control.

We grow from this in terms of how we are inspired and how we inspire others, both as people and as business leaders. This becomes contagious; I have seen it in action time and again.

## 2. USE THE POWER OF ENGAGEMENT

For me, the fundamental value the new breed of leader (the one that has 'grown up' over the past five years) is delivering, is an engaged workforce. If you create this, then you have happy, productive, motivated people who are delivering over and above what is expected, every day, for your customers.

This generates greater customer satisfaction, more purchases and higher profits. It's a fact – just look at the reports from the likes of Gallup, Deloitte and PWC. From this, the business can grow, and growth provides opportunities for development and career progression for staff, plus enhanced productivity and profit for the bottom line. So ignore the naysayers and know that an engaged, motivated, values-driven workforce can be unstoppable and that the potential is limitless.

## 3. FOCUS ON PRODUCTIVITY WITH A PURPOSE

How can an organisation be productive and successful if its people don't feel motivated and engaged to do their best and go the extra mile to meet shared goals? There is no greater evidence that learning and development leads to dynamic outcomes in terms of customer experience and therefore productivity. While productivity is vital in delivering a product or service, if your people can see the link between their own role and the values of the business and its overall mission, it becomes all the more powerful.

## 4. MAKE CORPORATE SOCIAL RESPONSIBILITY SUSTAINABLE AND ENGAGING

Many studies show that people are not motivated by money, but by emotion – by feeling good and doing well. The same should be true for business objectives and I believe businesses can have the best of both worlds, establishing more sustainable, charitable ways of working without compromising profit and growth (but, in fact, boosting them for the long term).

Corporate social responsibility (CSR) can benefit businesses in a number of ways, and if communities also benefit, it's a win-win situation. At a basic level, encouraging staff to take part in CSR initiatives boosts morale, costs very little and makes employees feel they (and their employer) are giving something back to others. Staff shouldn't be coerced into taking part, but inspired to volunteer through effective internal communications.

This connects to both innovation and engagement. On the innovation side, people can be allowed to be creative and to come up with exciting new CSR ideas. This helps them develop qualities such as project management, team building and empathy.

## 5. DEVELOP THE NEXT GENERATION OF LEADER

Embrace a new generation entering the workplace. Youth and fresh knowledge will help your organisation, to grow. We should all be training our replacements and preparing the next wave of leaders.

I believe very much in the idea of an inclusive company culture based on shared values and a shared mission, where everyone is engaged and working together under the same ethos. In my opinion, the belief that generations Y and Z should be treated differently from their predecessors (in other words, their colleagues), counteracts this. Why do we, as employers, put our recruits into boxes, only to spend years attempting to get them out again?

In an intergenerational workplace, the greatest opportunity for employers is to acknowledge what can and cannot be changed and then align people towards common goals, while allowing them to be themselves. Business success is a journey. Just as you were faced with challenges and took risks, you owe it to others to allow them to do the same. Don't be afraid to work with those who know more than you, and at the same time, look for potential in others who will grow through working with you.

## AND REMEMBER – OPERATIONAL EXCELLENCE IS NOT THE SAME AS STRATEGY

Sometimes, I think we misunderstand the difference between operational excellence and strategic leadership. The former is 'the people stuff' done well: engagement, productivity and a free-flowing talent pipeline.

The latter is putting in place the various elements of this and moulding it into long-term sustainable growth and innovation – not just for 'HR' but for the whole organisation.

Creating your strategy entails adopting a unique position, involving different sets of activities. It is worth referring to Michael Porter's classic book, *Competitive Strategy: What is Strategy,* for guidance. You must choose what to do, and what not to do, ensuring your strategy fits with the company's objectives. Operational excellence means doing something better than your competitors. The same can be true of excellence in leadership and building your framework: get the basics right, achieve operational excellence and then unveil your show-stopper.

## THE FRAMEWORK

I think about building strategy frameworks as a formula. Each leader and every organisation will have their own formula, so I'm not going to be prescriptive and tell you what you should put in it – that's for you to decide. But the following section outlines how a simple formula – or foundation – can become a framework, which can then become a strategy when you add layers and colours to it.

When it comes to developing a strategy for people – who are at the core of business success – there are three fundamental questions to consider:

1. **Attraction** – how are you going to recruit the highest calibre of people into your organisation and get them started on the road to success in your company?

2. **Growth** – how will you develop your people and enable them to perform to the best of their ability?

3. **Deliver** – how you can engage your people with the values and mission of your business, motivate them to be productive and offer great service to your customers, and empower them to innovate and grow your business towards world-class performance and profitability?

This is a fundamental framework, but it would look something like this:

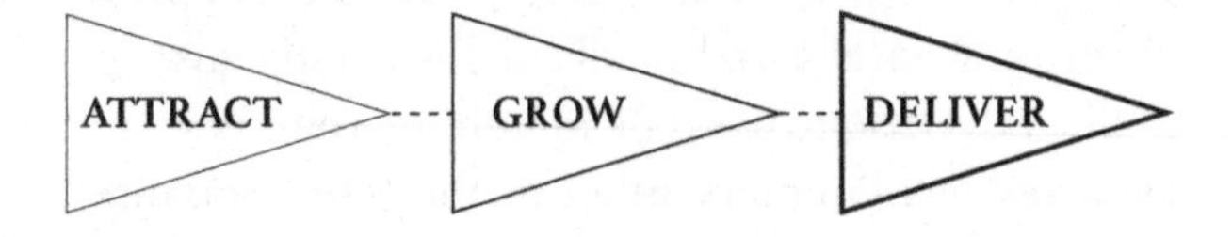


So, delving a bit deeper, you can build on this, by putting the right components in place, under each part of the framework. This is how the strategy will grow.

ATTRACT

- **Aspiration:** how can you position your organisation – whether a start-up, large corporate or a department within a business – as a place where people want to work? What is your employee value proposition (what do you offer existing staff)? What can you offer your recruits? What sets you apart from the competition?

- **Branding:** how can you clearly communicate your corporate values to potential employees? How do you market yourself as a great place to work? Do you have a clear employer brand? Is your organisation seen as a fun place to work? Are you regarded as a traditional employer? Are there negative perceptions of your brand that need to be addressed? Are you perceived as an organisation in which employees would succeed?

- **Recruitment:** how will you promote your jobs? Do you use recruitment engines, social media, print advertising, viral social media or PR campaigns, online advertising, word of mouth, recruitment agencies, head hunters, other methods or a mixture of these methods?

- **Assessment and selection:** how will people apply for jobs with you? Have you carried out market research to ascertain the most efficient ways of attracting applications? Do you have a recruitment page on your website? Will applicants send a CV or will you ask them to fill in a form? Will there be preliminary tests?

- **Interviewing:** how will you welcome applicants at interview? How will the interview process work? Do you have a plan in place to engage people with your business from their first interview? Will the process be formal or informal? How many interviews will be required? Will you carry out psychometric testing? Will you use metrics to ensure potential hires share your corporate values? How can you ensure your recruitment methods are effective and in line with the mission and values of the business?

- **Offer:** how will you offer the recruit a role (for example, via email, a phone call, face-to- face?) How will you start preparing them for the role before they start? Will they be sent an induction pack or invited to meet colleagues in advance? What employee engagement initiatives will you adopt to get them excited about starting and help them to 'hit the ground running' from their first day?

GROW

- **Onboarding:** how will you commence development, performance management, engagement and training from day one? Do you have job descriptions in place so employees and line managers can measure performance?

- **Enablement and development:** how will you understand the development needs of your people?

How can you make sure they know all there is to know about their roles so they can use their talents to deliver excellent work? What tools do they need to be fully enabled and empowered in their roles? How will future leaders be developed from day one and beyond? What will you do to implement sustainable development (long-terms plans rather than short-term gains)?

- **Talent management:** how will you ensure your people are on a career trajectory via which they will be developed, educated and promoted according to the values of your business, throughout their time with you? What is your current approach to succession planning?

- **Employee engagement:** I love this definition, coined by engagement experts Purple Cubed: "What will you do to ensure the right people are in the right roles, exceeding expectations, enthusiastically?"

## DELIVER

- **Customer service:** how can you ensure that all members of your team are working towards a goal of delighting customers with great service and/or products and impressing stakeholders with healthy profits?

- **Employee Engagement:** what initiatives do you have in place to keep employees motivated in their roles, producing great work, being productive as well as understanding and living the values and culture of your business?

- **Collaboration:** how are you developing teams and breaking down silos in your business, to get people working together, sharing ideas and solving problems as a group?

- **Empowerment and innovation:** how are you giving your people the freedom and opportunity to come up with new ideas, take responsibility for their own work and take pride in going the extra mile for the good of your business?

- **Goals and objectives:** what measures have you put in place? Will you use a balanced scorecard? How do you identify and impact upon strategic objectives? Can this information be used within future planning exercises?

## KNOW YOUR CONSTITUENTS

Your constituents could be the owners, shareholders, the board, employees, customers or other stakeholders. Each of these groups is different and each has varying interests, so a framework that leads to an effective strategy for one group will not necessarily be effective for another. And if your framework doesn't align with your constituents, you'll have a problem putting it into action.

So when doing things that work well on the people or product side, it's important to adopt an holistic perspective, not only considering the specific constituents you are targeting but also how your initiative, strategy or innovation might impact other constituents. Nowadays, the things we do have some kind of impact on all constituents. It's easier to consider these things from the beginning and plan for the eventualities than to try to tackle them mid-flow.

For example, a new CSR initiative clearly impacts upon an organisation's owners (their reputation) and its employees (the actions taken), but it's also important to consider how it effects customers and suppliers. How do they fit in? Will the initiative disrupt anything for them? Do you need to engage them?

# Over *to* YOU:

*How can you build a framework for:*
- *Your style of leadership*
- *Your current job / role*
- *Your next plan of action*

*Use this space to jot down your thoughts. Use some of the questions from the previous pages to help you frame your thinking.*

# *Chapter* SIX

# Chapter 6

## How do you bring your framework and strategy to life?

The previous chapter explored how to create a framework for your strategy, in order to build the foundations for what you are setting out to achieve. We will now consider how you can implement that strategy, bringing it to life and executing it flawlessly.

This, of course, is one of the hardest things to do. Too many people go out there and say: "Behold! Here is my strategy. I'm going to make it happen now." Ummm… how and when, exactly? Who will make it happen and how much will that cost?

## DON'T FORGET – TIME IS YOUR FRIEND

Time is about taking stock of what you've done and what you're doing and using this to inform your actions. The best thing about the past is that it's in the past. Think about the time you've had so far – what have you learned? What talents have you developed? What decisions have you made? Why? If you take all that knowledge you can use it in any job.

The beautiful thing about a new job or switching roles is that you get to reinvent yourself every time. You can start a new job with renewed confidence, a new style or a new focus.

When you start a new role, you have a unique opportunity to take stock, to assess your talents, skill-sets, leadership style. Take note of these and don't decide too quickly what you want to create next. I once took up a new role and, in the fourth week, I went to my leader with a load of ideas. He told me to stop and said he didn't want any ideas until I'd been at the company for six months. This was a great piece of advice because I paused and then continued to take stock. When I think back on those original ideas, I now know they would have spelled disaster.

Even at entry level, you can take stock of who you report to, your trajectory and so on. If you don't have time to do this, you cannot build a sustainable foundation.

There is far too much pressure on leaders to make decisions in their first 30 or even 100 days. Lots of leadership books have been written under the false assumption that leaders who don't make their mark on an organisation within the first 100 days have failed. I completely disagree with that. My advice would be to let yourself be known within the first 100 days. Make an impact with your personality, your presence, your relationships – these will be key. Take counsel from colleagues because these relationships will enable you to put your strategies in place when the time comes. People want to make a difference – but you'll never get these first months back again. You can hit the ground running but use this time to ask 'stupid' questions, understand the business, think about innovations and lay the foundations of your strategy. Don't try to do too much or you'll be seen as an over-enthusiastic loose cannon.

## PUSH THE BOUNDARIES

If you're reading this book and you're already months or years into your role, it's true that it's much harder to be innovative and creative in strategy planning at this stage, than if you're just starting a new job. But you could push the boundaries of your role. Think about the extra responsibilities you might be able to take on and don't be afraid to broaden your 'job description'. Of course, there will be core elements of your role that you must fulfil, but you can still create new opportunities; you're not bound to a piece of paper.

Let's take HR: the new breed of people leader is not limited to human resources, their remit encompasses 'culture', which embodies many more elements of the business, including customer service, CSR, facilities and even marketing. This means that rather than wearing a straightforward 'HR hat', they are likely to be juggling a variety of hats.

The profession of people leadership is always evolving and changing and you could explore other related departments in order to find opportunities for adding value.

Think about some of the roles in your business you'd like to know more about and investigate whether you could contribute in any way.

## EDUCATION, EDUCATION, EDUCATION

The key to executing strategy successfully is creating awareness around it: educating your teams and telling people about what's going on. This is where the work you've done in building relationships, mentioned earlier in the chapter, is going to pay dividends.

If you have your strategic plan and it is made up of a variety of different facets, you will need to spend some time running a roadshow: getting it out there and ensuring people understand it. For instance, if you're planning a new engagement strategy, talk to people about how it will look in your company, how it will make sense; use specific examples relating to your company and your industry and bring it to life for your people.

When you invest time in communication and education, you'll gain buy-in. This could take a week or it could take three months. It depends on the number of people you have to reach and how many levels of the business need to buy into your strategy. You have to factor in the time. If you launch something in the US, it could be finished in a month; in Italy, it could take a year. Some cultures are keen to get things going, whereas, in other regions, you will need to translate a proposal into the journey of the company, rather than shoehorn a strategy into place. Once you've considered the likely timescale, then and only then, will you be in a position to execute a strategy.

When I launch something, I tend to have meetings with people at various levels of the business. When we're rolling things out, I want there to be champions at all levels, who have had the initiative explained to them in advance and will be able to ensure the strategy is lived throughout the business, to the extent that when we announce it, they already know what it entails and will be our champions within the audience.

When we introduce something, it will be launched at executive level, then general management level, then to committees, followed by the rest of the staff. You need to have senior buy-in – but you'll need buy-in at all levels to ensure that something takes root and works. Everyone has to be on board.

## FROM INNOVATION TO IMPLEMENTATION

If you type 'definition of innovation' into any search engine, you'll be met with in the region of 285,000,000 articles, all offering up slightly different takes on what the perfect innovation framework looks like.

But before you get carried away with 'innovating' I urge you to think about why you're innovating. A fatal error made by businesses is focusing on one big innovation initiative but not following through on it, or implementing it properly.

For innovation to be successful, you need to ensure that the innovation makes sense in your business. Why do you want to innovate? Is it to gain competitive advantage or to be more efficient? Once you have decided why, it's about how you define it – your definition of innovation.

For example, the only true luxury in life is time. It's the one thing you can change (in order to receive more, or less, of it), unlike gravity or the laws of the world. Therefore, I define innovation as anything that offers a creative way of being more efficient and giving people more time to engage with customers. Engaging with customers creates loyalty which is fundamental to a business. If an idea shaves a mere three seconds off a process, then to me, you have succeeded in the innovation mission.

Once you have your definition, it's about making sure you gain the right insight – insight that identifies a true business need:

- Challenge the status quo: try and look past conventional thinking to gain fresh perspectives and identify areas for improvement.

- Identify all stages that have led you to an insight, spotting opportunities to adapt and magnify the idea.

- Generate ideas to solve an issue that would be impossible, immoral or illegal and then consider ways of making them realistic.

Having said that, every time you come up with an innovation, the key thing is to think back through this book and work through the steps of your framework to make sure you can plan it and make it a success. Does it fit with your company values and purpose? Do you and the business have the skills and talents to make it a success?

If you can devise solutions to any potential problems, then the time has come to build the framework for your innovation (as outlined in chapter five): strategise, educate, communicate, ignite, and finally, implement.

## MY TOP TIPS FOR INNOVATION:

- *Think outside of the box and be open to new approaches.*
- *Be curious and eager to learn; ask questions.*
- *Take risks and identify creative solutions.*
- *Encourage sharing of ideas to create the spirit of innovation.*
- *Find ways to anticipate trends.*
- *Seek opportunities to improve continuously.*

## WHAT GETS MEASURED GETS DONE

Only when people buy into your plan can its implementation run smoothly.

The final step is monitoring and measuring the success of your strategy as it rolls out. This will allow you to go back and tweak it, as necessary.

Just because you've developed a proposal doesn't mean it'll be your final strategy. Too many people think "I've written a plan, the board have accepted it; I HAVE to make it work." That's rubbish. If you need to change it – change it.

# Over *to* YOU:

*Use the following few pages to jot down some thoughts about the strategies you're working on in your current role. With whom do you need to build better relationships? How should you communicate your ideas and from whom do you need buy in? How could you better monitor and measure the strategies your business already has in place?*

# *Chapter* SEVEN

# Chapter 7

## What do you want to achieve?

In business, one-hit wonders – like the music artists whose pop anthems are relegated to cheesy wedding discos – are the strategies you'll have implemented that have a lot of initial 'bang'... but fizzle out. They make a good first impression but lack longevity.

Sometimes, you need them for a morale boost or a marketing push – but these one-hit wonders cannot be part of your strategy. If you have sustainability in mind, you'll be able to avoid them, and that's what I'd like to talk about in this chapter.

According to the *FT*, business sustainability is defined as managing the triple bottom line – a process by which companies manage their financial, social and environmental risks, obligations and opportunities. These three impacts are sometimes referred to as "profits, people and planet".

Businesses, regardless of the sector, region or industry within which they operate, surely have one thing in common: the desire to grow and generate significant profit margins.

Some, of course, enjoy more success than others, but what if I were to tell you that caring for the environment is a means of business growth? You might think I was going slightly mad. Surely, when business leaders talk about CSR, they're just doing it to generate some positive PR or to fulfil a legal obligation?

You'd be wrong. I believe that CSR is a visionary, sustainable business strategy – and what's more, I can demonstrate it: wildlife cannot live in a polluted ecosystem and businesses cannot grow in a derelict environment.

As I outline in chapter five, sustainability relates to how we do business: demonstrating a commitment to health and safety, people, communities, education, charitable efforts and the environments in which we operate. At a basic level, encouraging staff to take part in CSR and sustainability initiatives boosts morale, costs a business very little and makes employees feel they (and their employer) are giving something back to others. Staff shouldn't be coerced, but inspired to volunteer through effective internal communications.

This connects to both innovation and engagement. On the innovation side, people can be allowed to be creative and come up with exciting new sustainability ideas – they also develop qualities such as project management, team building and empathy.

The World Commission on Environment and Development (WCED) has suggested that achieving sustainability will require an approach that de-emphasises growth and explicitly embraces environmental and social goals as the key dimensions of development. Many studies show that people are not primarily motivated by money, but by emotion – feeling good and doing well. The same should be true for business objectives and I believe businesses can have the best of both worlds, establishing more sustainable, charitable ways of working which don't compromise profit and growth, but build on them for the long-term.

Ultimately then, this connects your strategy to your purpose, so when you're planning your career goals, you have the opportunity to think about what you're doing, both in terms of being an inspirational leader now and in the future.

## CAREER GOALS

Everyone should have a career goal, no matter how much success they have already achieved – whether that's moving up the corporate ladder or achieving a certain position and securing stability that enables you to prioritise what's important to you. I've worked with plenty of people whose ultimate goal was to became an assistant director of HR. They wanted to stay at this level because while they were keen to work hard and do well, their higher priority was family.

When setting career goals, you need to decide where you are heading. It's not as simple as working out whether you're a 'leader' or a 'follower' because you can take the lead in a lot of different things, whether or not you're a strategic driver. However, once you have an idea of the direction in which you'd like to move, both at work and in life, you'll be in a position to identify your career goals - short, medium and longer term.

**Over to YOU:**

*Take some time to think about your priorities – have you decided on your direction and 'programmed your personal sat nav'?*

## A NEW BREED

As I explained in my introduction, world-class 'people strategy' is being spearheaded by a new breed of leader. Their strategy is creative, disruptive, forward thinking, sustainable, fiercely competitive – but equally collaborative.

I stressed that the leader of the future brings with them innovation, empathy, assertiveness, astuteness and, perhaps most importantly, a sense of humour. I hope you've read this far because you want to be part of this new breed.

However, the future of this new type of leader remains uncertain.

The fall-out from the 2008 financial crisis and the volatile, complex environment within which we have become 'comfortably uncomfortable', has meant that people imperatives such as talent management, strategic workforce planning and performance management have risen up the priority lists of executive boards. However, these initiatives have also received great scrutiny, as businesses look to secure their all-important return on investment.

As such, and explained earlier in the book, people leaders need to prove their worth. They need to challenge and provoke the business. They need to raise the bar considerably in terms of demonstrating the value of their strategies and interventions.

A common fault is thinking about people strategy and leadership as a 'function' or a 'set of activities'. People leaders need to ask themselves whether they are approaching people strategy from a leadership perspective: are they looking at 'best practice models' or are they looking at their own business to find out what to adapt?

For example, how can a sales department be successful if people strategy doesn't contribute to careful talent selection; where do we hire gifted sales professionals? Retaining and motivating high-performing sales professionals also requires input from HR, including bespoke motivational strategies.

Too many functions are still fire fighting against performance management and administrative bureaucracy, meaning they get tarred with the 'negative' brush. It's the way the business is set up. Sometimes, a cultural shift is needed before the new breed of leader can be taken seriously.

There remains a rippling undercurrent of negativity in some circles and I believe this to be down to the inability to evolve leadership approaches in an ever-changing world.

The good news is that, as the new breed of leader is beginning to proves their worth to the board, customers and employees, it feels as if there has been a seismic shift in how leadership is viewed in business and a growing realisation that it can truly add value to the bottom line.

This also speaks to the important relationship the people leader has with the general manager or even the CEO in terms of providing a voice of reason, insight and knowledge that informs the latter about their organisation's capabilities to achieve goals that align to the strategic plan. A people leader can narrow the gap between what we are and what we want to become because we need people to get there.

The key is to worry less about how we brand ourselves and whether we should be 'people' or 'HR' leaders and focus more on creating clear strategies that render us true business partners, able to deliver tangible results for the organisation as a whole. Not every marketing person can be a financier and not every finance person can work in operations – that's a fact of life. The secret to success is to break down silos and collaborate with colleagues in other departments, until people strategy is as important to them as it is to you; until your peers from other disciplines understand the value of people strategy.

## FROM PEOPLE LEADER TO CEO: THE FUTURE OF SUSTAINABLE LEADERSHIP

What is the future for aspiring leaders? Where can your career go? When you've done all you can in a role, what is the next step for a successful leader? Just because you're currently in a particular role doesn't mean you have to stay in it. It could constitute the beginning of a beautiful career you never thought you would have. The field of HR will help you to develop plenty of transferable skills.

HR leaders often work closely with colleagues from other disciplines, for example, liaising with PR or marketing departments on branding or raising the profile of new roles. This experience could easily set up an HR professional for a transition into a more marketing-focused position. (And if you're not in HR at the moment – there's no reason why you couldn't move into it).

Most high-flying people directors eventually move into portfolio work, take up non-executive roles, provide consultancy, become entrepreneurs or move to HR positions within different settings or sectors that provide them with a fresh challenge. I'm very much of the opinion that leadership is a transferrable skill and that great people leaders can adapt their style to any industry. But if people are an organisation's greatest asset, surely it's the people who have embraced leadership throughout their careers who will make the best MDs or CEOs of the future?

People leaders have been given responsibility for managing business transformation, which is, in itself, a key focus of any forward-thinking CEO – perhaps as big a priority as balancing the books, in strategic terms. They understand the complexities of the business right down to the minutiae. And running an HR department is more complex than managing other departments – it's like running a business in itself.

As people strategy evolves and the function attracts an influx of talented young HR careerists who are genuinely interested in, and adept at, business, these people will move back and forth from line to leadership, gaining the necessary profit and loss experience. However, it's vital that people leaders do not take for granted their trusted position as confidant to the CEO, the business and to its people. With trust comes responsibility.

The recession has certainly sharpened the people focus. HR issues are now firmly seen as business issues. So while I don't believe 'pure HR' can equip anyone to run a business, there is no reason why people leaders who have led divisions, and understand the nuts and bolts of business, cannot bridge the seemingly 'unbridgeable gap' from HR to the CEO's office.

Surely it's time for further debate around this issue and I would be keen to hear your thoughts and opinions.

I think it's pretty exciting. You can find me on LinkedIn, so connect and share your ideas.

## THINK ABOUT A CAREER PATH

When I started out in my career, I initially worked at the fryer at McDonalds – and I became the team leader. In hotels, I started off as a room cleaner; I never expected to be a vice president, yet here I am.

In every job I have ever had – whether I loved or hated it – I have learned something. In my earliest roles I found my voice and learned to be courageous and in junior positions. I came to understand time management, values and cultural awareness (not to mention the importance of being a little afraid). In more senior roles I learned about legalities, dealing with difficult people, international thinking, engagement and collaboration.

I'm still learning every day and I'd advise you to think about what you're learning too – and to do your job like you're not afraid to lose it. Otherwise, what's the point? You would have lost your purpose.

The opportunities are certainly there for the taking, but I think too many people are kicking off their careers by setting out a five- to ten-year path. It's just as important to think about 'now' and what good looks like in the present. Sometimes, it's quite refreshing not to worry about your career path, to love your job and work in the moment.

The minute I stopped worrying about progressing my career, it progressed. I paid attention but didn't obsess. It worked for me and could work for you too.

When I started my career in housekeeping, I knew I didn't want to clean rooms, but what I learned in those six months was team working, how to build relationships with co-workers, confidence, and time management. I took away skills that prepared me for my next job.

I'd urge you to avoid mapping out your career in its entirety – you may not be in the right job right now, but you could still learn skills that will give you something extra to use in future. Think differently, flip things on their head. Consider what you've got access to and how that could then be applied in different roles, outside of a traditional career path.

Slow down and think about it. You'll find you actually progress faster because you've acquired more skills. I know this is surprisingly hard to do because it's so easy to get bogged down in the turbulence of "this job sucks", but try to look deeper into your situation and to view it more positively. Harness your determination, values and openness to learn and see the bigger picture.

We consistently talk about "talent strategy"; for me, it's important to understand that not everyone can do every job. Your current focus may change in less than five years. Your priorities will evolve, so it's worth coming back to this chapter again and again, looking at your list of priorities, drivers and ambitions, and rethinking them.

# Over *to* YOU:

*What have you learnt so far in your career? What are your priorities for the future. Consider your answers and jot them down here, off the top of your head. What are your drivers right now? How flexible are you when it comes to your career and your ambitions?*

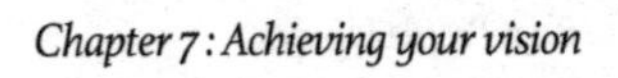

# *Chapter* EIGHT

# Chapter 8

## What will be your legacy?

Your legacy in any role will be characterised by what people say about you after you leave. The decisions you make today will influence the future of your organisation and your role as a sustainable leader – especially when it comes to policy and procedures; for example, terminating contracts and so on. These will all have knock-on effects five years from now and could fundamentally alter the culture of your business.

## WHY IS IT IMPORTANT TO LEAVE A LEGACY?

Purpose must be paramount in terms of your legacy – you, as a leader, are in a position to lay foundations for the future of your business, so the long-term sustainability of the things you do should be a consideration when you are building your frameworks and strategies.

When you start a job, colleagues will tell you all about your predecessor. What will they say about you when you leave? With how many people will you be replaced?

I'd been in a role for eight years at one organisation and, when I left, four people took over the role of HR director within five years and it made me wonder… did I not set this up for success? Was the strategy I left unclear?

When it comes to legacy, the things you put in place – style, leadership, formula, strategy – will all be tested. Anyone can formulate great results when they're in a job because they're managing every step of the process. When you're not there, that's when your true legacy will be felt.

To me, an ideal legacy is to leave a sustainable operation; whether it takes your employer a day or a year to replace you, if the operation doesn't fall apart in that time, you've left a good legacy.

Every formula and strategy has to be 'living', so it can change in line with law, politics, environments, society, people, leaderships and boards. It has to be a living document. If the CEO changes and everything changes with it, your legacy is weak. People will come in with their own ideas, but if you've set a strong foundation, new ideas can be incorporated.

You shouldn't be offended if you leave a role and your successor does things differently. I was once succeeded by someone who did completely different things to me, because she had a different style and it was a different time. I know I made the right decisions for the time I was there – good practices and sustainability – but the economy changed and she had to make her strategy 'live'. I hope I gave her a sufficiently strong platform, that enabled her to make changes easily. You're kidding yourself if you think things will never be 'as good' when you leave. That's not a helpful way to think, as a leader – to believe your way is the only way.

## PAYING IT FORWARD

For me, 'paying it forward' is the crux of a legacy. Sometimes I don't think we, as leaders, realise how much knowledge and experience we have.

Recently, I've been thinking a lot about global strategies. I've come to realise that my knowledge is transferable; it took me 23 years into a career to realise how much I know.

I acknowledge that I have done a good job in promoting my assistants, that I have a great track record in terms of delivering successful strategies. Now I feel I have an opportunity to share the knowledge and bring other people on the journey with me, so they can see what is possible (hence the purpose of this book).

Remember, paying it forward is less about 'you' and much more about others. You're never bigger than the brand you work for and I think, in leadership, it's easy to think you are. When thinking about your career path and imagining your legacy, think about how you can collaborate, how you can share with others and how you can enhance both your career and the careers of others.

## TO CLOSE: YOUR ROLE IN ENHANCING THE LEADERSHIP OF TOMORROW

If you take away just one thing from this book, I hope it will be that purpose, culture, talent and engagement should take centre stage in the workforce of the future. In simple terms, I believe that where talented individuals – whether leaders, or members of the wider workforce – are brought into the right company culture, share the values and mission of a business, and receive dedicated training and development, they can thrive. They will inspire their colleagues, delight their customers and play their part in generating sustainable growth.

This is a journey that starts before a person even joins a company and continues throughout their career. The key is to listen to your people; to ensure they share your beliefs and culture; are recognised for the great work they produce; understand their role in building the company; and have a clear progression path for their career.

How can an organisation be productive and successful if its people are not motivated and engaged to do their best and to go the extra mile to achieve shared goals? For me, the fundamental value of the new breed of people-centric leader is an engaged workforce. If you achieve this during your career, in line with your framework, and empower others through your legacy, continue this work and pay it forward, we will have happy, productive, motivated people – now and in the future – who will deliver over and above what is expected of them, every day.

This generates greater customer satisfaction, more purchases and higher profits.

From this, businesses can grow, enhance their productivity and the bottom line, while their staff gain opportunities for development and career progression. An engaged, motivated, values-driven workforce can be unstoppable and its potential limitless.

# Over *to* YOU.

# About the Author

Eugenio Pirri is an award-winning hospitality stalwart with a career spanning over 25 years; beginning in rooms division and then food and beverage, before making the transition into human resources. As a vice president, people and organisational development for a global hotel management company, Eugenio is responsible for all aspects of Human Resources, Learning and Development, Employee and Guest Engagement, Innovation and Corporate Responsibility, working with all functions in the business to ensure our people are the cornerstone of every business decision.

In recent years, Eugenio's expertise in this field has been recognised by leading publications. He, and his team, have won more than 10 prestigious HR and business awards including the Gold Award at the HR Excellence Awards. Eugenio collected both HR Director of the Year and Reader's Choice HR Director in 2015. He is also named as one of the most influential HR Director's in the world.

Eugenio lives in Little Venice, London though often travels to far and wide destinations instilling his leadership words of wisdom in businesses around the globe.

You can connect with him via:

**@eugeniopirri**

**https://uk.linkedin.com/in/epirri17**